CAN I FEED IT?

HODDER
Wayland

an imprint of Hodder Children's Books

New Experiences

Are We There Yet? My First Holiday
Can I Feed It? My First Pet
I Want That Room! Moving House
I'm Still Important! A New Baby
Open Wide! My First Trip to the Dentist
Say Aah! My First Visit to the Doctor
Where's My Peg? My First Day at School
Where's My Present? My First Party

Published in Great Britain in 2000 by Hodder Wayland,
an imprint of Hodder Children's Books
© Copyright 2000 Hodder Wayland

This paperback edition published in 2001

Editor: Jason Hook
Designer: Tessa Barwick

A Catalogue record for this book is available from the British Library.

ISBN 0 7500 3031 3

Printed and bound in Italy by G. Canale & C.Sp.A., Turin

Hodder Children's Books
A division of Hodder Headline Limited
338 Euston Road, London NW1 3BH

CAN I FEED IT?

My First Pet

Written by Jen Green

Illustrated by Mike Gordon

HODDER
Wayland

an imprint of Hodder Children's Books

All my friends have pets. Kirsty from next door has a cat.

James keeps gerbils. Ben has budgies.

I don't want a cat, a gerbil or a budgie. I just want a puppy.

Dad said dogs are a lot of work. You have to feed them, brush them and take them for walks every day.

'I'll do all that,' I said.
'I really want a puppy.'

Mum said pets are a bother. Dogs and cats get fleas.

They also jump up and make your clothes hairy.

She told me that they leave muddy pawprints everywhere. 'I'll help clear up,' I said.

At last Mum and Dad said yes!
I helped Mum fence the garden.

We went to the pet shop and bought a bed, bowl, collar and lead, and some food.

We went to a rescue centre.
There were lots of grown-up
dogs there that needed a home.

And in one pen, there was the most cute and bouncy puppy you ever saw.

At first our puppy was scared of its new home, and hid beneath the sofa.

Later our puppy got brave and came to play with me. It even met the cat from next door.

'Can I feed it?' I asked. 'You can feed *her*,' said Mum. Our new puppy gulped down all her dinner.

We decided to
call her Lucky.

Dad was right – puppies are a lot of work. Lucky learned to wee outdoors, but she dug up the flower-bed.

We had to give
her a bath.

Mum was right, too – pets are a bother sometimes. Lucky chewed our slippers.

She dragged Mum's washing in the mud, and chased next door's cat.

But Lucky
became our
friend, too. Who jumps
for joy when we get home?
Who comes for walks with us?

22

Who licks my face when I feel sad?
Who else, but our new puppy!

We took Lucky to dog-training classes. She learned to come, sit, stay, heel, lie down and fetch.

Now she's a good dog, and does what she's told – mostly.

One day we took Lucky to a dog show. She didn't win best of breed or funniest tail.

But she did win
first prize for
cleverest puppy!

Puppies grow up
fast. Lucky's quite a
grown-up dog now.

If Mum and Dad say yes, perhaps one day she'll have puppies of her own.

Notes for parents and teachers

This book introduces children to the experience of having pets. Parents or teachers who read the book with children may find it useful to stop and discuss issues as they come up.

Having a pet is a big decision. Pets bring changes to all family members, including young children. Pets can be very rewarding and great fun. They can help children learn to be unselfish and to consider others. But owning a pet such as a dog or cat is also a big responsibility, and a lot of work. Dogs, in particular, need frequent exercise and enjoy having company. They must be walked every day and not be left alone for too long.

The financial aspect of owning a pet should also be considered. Keeping a dog or cat is expensive. As well as food, there are vets' bills to consider, and the cost of boarding the animal at a kennel or cattery when you go away.

When choosing a pet, make sure that the animal is calm with children. Never leave very young children alone with a new pet.

Animals from rescue centres, in particular, need patience, love and understanding. Any new pet will take a while to settle into its new home.

In class, children who have pets might like to talk about their own experiences. They could write a story about their own pets, using the book as a framework. Or they could make up and illustrate a story about a best or worst pet. The stories could be put together to make a class book.

The experience of getting a pet may introduce unfamiliar words, including: rescue centre, dog-training, heel, breed, canine, feline, bitch, mongrel, veterinary, grooming, kennel, cattery. Make a list of all the new words and discuss what they mean.

Use this book for teaching literacy

This book can help you in the literacy hour in the following ways:

✓ Children can write simple stories linked to personal experience using the language of the text in this book as a model for their own writing. (Year 1, Term 3: Non-fiction writing composition.)

✓ Children can look through the book and try to locate verbs with past and present tense endings. (Year 1, Term 3: Word recognition, graphic knowledge and spelling.)

✓ Use of speech bubbles shows a different way of presenting text. (Year 2, Term 2: Sentence construction and punctuation.)

Books to read

Daddy, Could I Have an Elephant? by Jake Wolf, illustrated by Marylin Hafner (Greenwillow Books, 1996). Tony wants a pet and asks his dad for an elephant. But his father thinks an elephant would be too difficult to keep. A pony would leave hoofprints on the furniture, and a sheep might keep everyone awake at bedtime. Finally, Tony settles on a puppy.

Josh by Andrew and Janet McLean (Allen and Unwin, 1997) Josh is a naughty spaniel who likes to be in on everything. He's also the best friend a boy or girl could have.

How to Look After Your Cat/Dog/Hamster/Rabbit by Colin and Jacqui Hawkins (Walker Books, 1996) Practical tips on pet care for the young pet-owner, illustrated with funny cartoons.